14.95

W9-ATF-081

ARIZONA

Rennay Craats

Published by Weigl Publishers Inc.
123 South Broad Street, Box 227
Mankato, MN   56002
USA
Web site: http://www.weigl.com

Library of Congress Cataloging-in-Publication Data

Craats, Rennay
    Arizona / Rennay Craats.
      p. cm. -- (A kid's guide to American states)
    Includes index.
    ISBN 1-930954-77-8 (lib.bdg.)
     1. Arizona--Juvenile literature. [1. Arizona.] I. Title. II. Series.

F811.3 .C7 2001

2001017995

ISBN 1-930954-68-9 (pbk.)

Printed in the United States of America
1 2 3 4 5 6 7 8 9 10   05 04 03 02 01

Project Coordinator
Jennifer Nault
Substantive Editor
Leslie Strudwick
Copy Editor
Heather Kissock
Designers
Warren Clark
Terry Paulhus
Photo Researcher
Angela Lowen

Photograph Credits

Every reasonable effort has been made to trace ownership and to obtain permission to reprint copyright material. The publishers would be pleased to have any errors or omissions brought to their attention so that they may be corrected in subsequent printings.

Cover: Grand Canyon (Corbis Corporation), Turquoise (Wayne O. Brown–Miner and Cutter of Natural Morenci Turquoise); **Archive Photos:** 21T, 25T; **Arizona Diamondbacks:** 27BL; **Arizona Historical Foundation:** 18T, 18BL; **Arizona Office of Tourism / Chris Coe:** 3B, 4T, 6BR, 7BR, 9BR, 12B, 15T, 16T, 16B, 18BR, 19B, 20T, 20BR, 24B, 29R; **Bob and Suzanne Clemenz:** 3M, 5T, 7T, 8T, 12T, 20BL, 22T, 22BR, 22BL, 23T, 23B, 25BR, 26T; **Corbis Corporation:** 14T, 14BR; **Corel Corporation:** 3T, 8BL, 10T, 10BL, 10BR, 11ML, 13M, 16MR, 26ML, 29L; **M. Corrado / Bruce Bennett Studios:** 27MR; **EyeWire Corporation:** 14BL; **Jessen Associates Inc.:** 21B; **Jessen Associates Inc. / R. Silberblatt:** 4BR, 6BL, 7BL, 8BR, 9T, 9BL, 26BR, 28R; **Drew Milsom:** 5BL; **Nevada Commission on Tourism:** 4ML; **PhotoDisc Corporation:** 15B, 25BL; **Monique de St. Croix:** 6T, 11T, 11B, 13T, 13B, 24T, 28L; **The UT Institute of Texan Cultures at San Antonio:** 17T, 17B; **Visuals Unlimited:** 19T.

CONTENTS

INTRODUCTION

Many people visit Arizona every year to hike in the Grand Canyon.

"The Grand Canyon State" was once considered a barren desert, but it has developed into one of the wealthiest states in the nation. Vast **irrigation** systems have transformed the dry desert soil into successful farmland, while the mild winters and hot summers attract so many people that Arizona is one of the country's fastest-growing regions. Between 1950 and 2000, the population increased seven-fold.

While ninety percent of the people live in the south of the state, the northern half contains some of the most breathtaking scenery in the country. The Grand Canyon, which inspired the state nickname, is one of the natural wonders of the world, but there are forty-seven other parks, monuments, and wildlife preserves to visit across this incredible state.

QUICK FACTS

The state gemstone is the turquoise. This stunning gemstone has been used to make jewelry in the state for centuries.

Arizona's state motto is *Ditat Deus*, which is Latin for "God Enriches."

With an area of 114,006 square miles, Arizona is the sixth-largest state in the United States.

The government owns or controls about seventy percent of the state's land.

Phoenix is the manufacturing, financial, tourist, and retirement center of Arizona. It is the largest city in Arizona, with about 1.1 million people.

Monument Valley lies entirely within the Navajo reservation on the Utah–Arizona border.

Getting There

Arizona is a nearly rectangular state located in the southwestern United States. It borders Utah to the north and New Mexico to the east. The Mexican state Sonora makes up Arizona's southern border. The Colorado River serves as the state's western border, with Nevada and California on the other side. Four Corners, at the northeast tip of Arizona, is where four states—Arizona, Utah, Colorado, and New Mexico—all meet at right angles.

Arizona has more than 54,000 miles of roads and highways that connect it to many other cities and states. Before 1959, parts of Arizona on the north side of the Colorado River were quite **isolated**. The Grand Canyon separated some areas from other parts of the state. A steel arch bridge was built near Glen Canyon Dam, linking the north to the south.

Arizona is better served by public transportation than much of the Southwest. There are more than 280 airports in the state. Phoenix's airport, Sky Harbor International, is the busiest airport in the state. It is also the seventh-busiest airport in the nation.

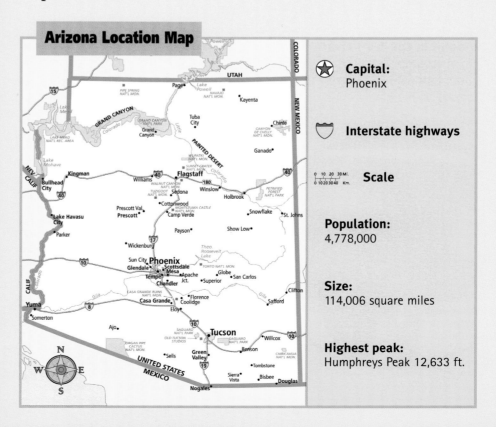

Arizona Location Map

Capital: Phoenix

Interstate highways

Scale

Population: 4,778,000

Size: 114,006 square miles

Highest peak: Humphreys Peak 12,633 ft.

More than 300,000 people spend their winters in Arizona's RV parks.

QUICK FACTS

The state's name is thought to have come from the Native-American word *arizonac*. It means "small spring."

Phoenix has served as the state capital since 1889.

Arizona is the only state in the country that does not participate in daylight saving time.

Temperatures in Phoenix can reach 110° Fahrenheit in the summer but Arizonans stay comfortable in air-conditioned homes, workplaces, and vehicles. In the winter, while much of the nation is shivering with cold, Arizona is blessed with pleasant temperatures. This makes the state an ideal winter getaway. A large number of retired senior citizens, called "snowbirds," drive south and spend their winters in Arizona. For instance, the summer population in the town of Quartzsite is about 2,000. In the winter, the snowbirds bump the population up to more than 1 million.

The state has many permanent senior citizen residents; the number of Arizonans in their eighties quadrupled from 1970 to 1990. Young people are also flocking to the state to enjoy its sunshine and opportunities.

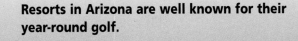

Resorts in Arizona are well known for their year-round golf.

Cathedral Rock is one of the most photographed landforms in the nation.

It took the Colorado River about 6 million years to carve out Arizona's most celebrated sight—the Grand Canyon. This heart-stopping **gorge** is 18 miles across at its widest point, more than 1 mile below the earth's surface at its deepest, and 277 miles long. Within the canyon there are impressive **mesas** and **buttes** formed by the action of water on the rocks. The layers of rock in the canyon tell the history of Arizona. Different kinds of limestone, sandstone, and shale are stacked like pancakes in the earth. Some of the fossils and deposits found in this area are hundreds of millions of years old.

The canyon, and part of the plateau surrounding it, is preserved as the Grand Canyon National Park. In the summer, about 6,000 cars arrive at the Grand Canyon's South Rim every day. People can explore this World Heritage Site by peering over the edge, hiking down into the canyon, or taking a bus tour along the rim. Others rent mules and ride down into the canyon. Visitors can fly over the canyon in helicopters and airplanes. Also, river rafters brave the Colorado River to observe the Grand Canyon from below.

The Grand Canyon is noted for its fantastic shapes and colors. Sunrise and sunset are the best times to view the canyon.

QUICK FACTS

The state fossil is **petrified** wood.

Arizona is the sixth largest state in the nation.

Arizona's state seal depicts its important economic activities, including mining and agriculture.

The state flag has thirteen red and yellow rays that represent the original thirteen colonies of the Union. A copper star in the center represents the state's major natural resource—copper. The blue bottom half of the flag represents liberty.

Not all of Arizona is dry and arid. Oak Creek Canyon is a lush paradise with gurgling rivers and pine forests.

LAND AND CLIMATE

Although most of Arizona's population live in desert areas, more than half of the state is mountain and plateau. There are three main land regions: the Colorado Plateau, the Transition Zone, and the Basin and Range region. The Colorado Plateau is a dry, flat semidesert region that covers northern Arizona. The Plateau ends with the steep rock wall of the Mogollon Rim. The Transition Zone is south of the Colorado Plateau. There are several mountain ranges in this thin strip of land, including the Mazatzal, Santa Maria, Sierra Ancha, and White ranges. The Basin and Range region, which covers most of the south and some of the west of Arizona, is very dry.

While average temperatures in the desert may not dip to below freezing for several years, winter temperatures in the mountains can fall to 0°F. The desert regions of the south and west receive very little rainfall, but the state's northern and eastern mountain ranges often receive 150 to 300 inches of snow per year.

Arizona's deserts experience large daily temperature changes. The deserts are often hot during the day, but can be very cold at night.

QUICK FACTS

Phoenix endures about ninety-one days a year when the mercury soars above 100°F.

Arizona is sprinkled with deserts. Northwestern Arizona is home to the Mojave Desert, the state's driest desert. In the northeast is the Great Basin Desert, and in the southeastern corner lies the Chihuahuan Desert. The cactus-filled Sonoran Desert covers the southern third of Arizona.

The highest temperature recorded in Arizona was 128°F in 1905. The coldest temperature was –40°F in 1971.

NATURAL RESOURCES

Arizona's first settlers were lured to the state by its wealth of minerals. Today, its natural resources remain important to the state's economy. Arizona is rich in copper, and the state mines about two-thirds of the nation's total of this resource. There are open-pit and underground copper mines in many parts of the state. Other key minerals in Arizona include gold, molybdenum, and silver.

Sand and gravel are mined in the state and are used in construction. Other natural resources important to the state include gypsum, quartz, coal, petroleum, and gemstones.

Water is a precious resource in the state. A system of canals was first established by the Native Americans hundreds of years ago. These canals are still used by Arizonan farmers for transporting water to irrigate crops. To conserve this resource, the government has established a water management program. Many dams, such as the giant Hoover Dam on the Nevada border, have been built to create reservoirs for water storage and to produce **hydroelectricity**.

Many rivers in Arizona do not flow year round.

QUICK FACTS

Molybdenum and vanadium are found in Arizona. They are used to harden steel.

Clay, bentonite, feldspar, iron, and salt are other natural resources found in Arizona.

In many Arizona farm budgets, water costs are the single highest expense. Virtually every acre of production agriculture in the state is irrigated.

Copper mining in Arizona began in Bisbee, in 1880.

PLANTS AND ANIMALS

The Teddy Bear Cholla looks soft and fuzzy from a distance, but its spines are barbed and sharp.

Seventy types of cacti grow in Arizona. The largest cactus in the country is the majestic saguaro that grows to a height of 50 feet and lives up to 200 years. The white blossom of this cactus is the state flower. Prickly pear, barrel, and organ-pipe cacti also grow in Arizona. Cacti thrive in the desert climate because they are able to store water in their stems and roots. Some bushes, including creosote and sagebrush, also store moisture.

The mountain areas boast an entirely different kind of plant life. Although Arizona is known for its desert land, about one-quarter of the state is thick with forests. The largest number of ponderosa pine trees in the country are found in Arizona's mountains. Aspen, cottonwood, blue spruce, and walnut trees are also found in the state.

QUICK FACTS

The paloverde is the state's official tree. The name is Spanish for "green stick," and refers to the color of the bark.

The mesquite tree is one of the state's most common desert trees.

More than 400 edible plants grow in the Sonoran Desert.

The largest member of the yucca family is the Joshua tree. It is dominant in the northwestern deserts.

Poppies and yucca flowers are common wildflowers in southern Arizona.

There are eleven different rattlesnake species in Arizona.

The Arizona trout is the state fish. The ringtail is the state mammal, the ridgenose rattlesnake is the state reptile, and the Arizona tree frog is the state amphibian.

The Kaibab Plateau in Arizona is the only place in the country where the white-tailed black Kaibab squirrel lives.

Arizona's collared lizards run on their hind legs when they are alarmed.

It takes hardy animals to live in some of the harsh areas of Arizona. Forty different kinds of lizards, including the poisonous Gila monster, roam the state. Scorpions and tarantulas inhabit the hotter areas. Rattlesnakes and coral snakes may be found slithering along the desert floor. The desert tortoise adds to the fascinating wildlife. It has extremely long nails which it uses to dig through desert sand to find shelter. Desert mule deer graze on cactus fruit in the winter and look for higher scrub forests for food in the summer.

In Arizona's grasslands, herds of pronghorn antelope share pastures with **domestic** cattle and sheep. White-tailed deer, elk, and mountain lions are found in the forests. Foxes, badgers, and wild pigs called javelinas all live on Arizona's varied land. In the sky, eagles soar near the mountains, and vultures circle the desert floor. Roadrunners and wild turkeys are also common sights.

The javelina eats grasses, fruits, and seeds, but its favorite food is prickly pear cactus.

Mountain lions are rarely seen in the wild. Still, they are the most common wild cat in North America.

The red rock of Cathedral Rock is caused by oxidation, which is the rusting of the iron in the rock.

TOURISM

Arizona has a booming tourism industry. People come to the state to visit the spectacular natural formations at the Grand Canyon. People also visit Monument Valley, Meteor Crater, and the Petrified Forest. Here, they can view gigantic fossilized trees that have turned to stone over 200 million years. The state also has the two largest reservations in the country, and visitors gather to see traditional Navajo and Tohono O'odham ceremonies, or to buy Native American arts and crafts.

Arizona's Wild West history is alive in towns like Tombstone. This town is the site of the famed gunfight at the O.K. Corral. Restored saloons and re-enactments give visitors a sense of the rough-and-ready lifestyles of the pioneers. Boot Hill Graveyard also gives visitors a chilling reminder of how wild the West really was. Rows of tombstones mark those who lost their lives during this rough period.

The mining town of Tombstone survived the decline in the silver-mining industry and earned the nickname "Town Too Tough To Die."

A network of canals, tunnels, and water pipelines covers the state.

INDUSTRY

The state has more than than 36 million acres of farmland, but only 5 percent of this land is used to grow crops. Most of the land is used to raise livestock, and cattle sales make up the largest source of income for farmers and ranchers annually. Arizona has about 822,000 cattle and 140,000 sheep.

Farming in Arizona is highly commercialized and industrialized. This is evident in the state's cotton fields. Arizona ranks sixth in the country for cotton production. The warm, sunny climate also makes Arizona an important fruit and vegetable producer, especially during the winter, when these items are in short supply. Miles of lemon, orange, and grapefruit groves line the desert.

More than half of Arizona's electric power is obtained from steam plants burning coal to generate power. About one-third of the state's power comes from nuclear plants west of Phoenix at Palo Verde. Hydroelectric plants create one-tenth of the state's power. Dams on the Colorado River provide water or power to one-tenth of Americans and three-quarters of Arizonans.

Arizona produces about 62 billion kilowatt hours of electricity every year.

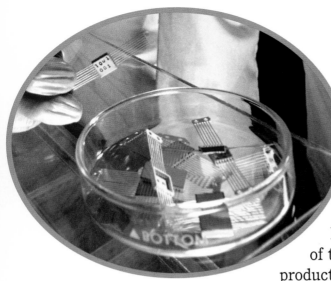

Arizona is a leading computer chip manufacturer.

GOODS AND SERVICES

About 16 percent of Arizona's economy is fueled by manufacturing. Most manufacturing plants are located in Phoenix and Tucson. Electronic goods are very important to this sector of the economy. About $1.3 billion worth of electronic products are produced in Arizona each year. Some manufacturers produce space vehicles and guided missiles for the government. Others produce aerospace equipment, televisions, and machinery. With the growth of the computer industry, Arizona manufacturers are making a variety of computer components. Computer software manufacturing is another rapidly growing industry in the state.

Arizonans can stay informed by reading any of the eighty magazines or the ninety newspapers published in the state. Twenty of these newspapers are dailies. *The Arizona Republic*, printed in Phoenix, has the highest circulation. Other popular papers include *The Arizona Daily Star* and *The Tucson Citizen*, which are both printed in Tucson.

QUICK FACTS

The electronics industry is a growing sector in Arizona's economy.

Arizona's first commercial radio station was KFAD. It sent out its first broadcast from Phoenix in 1922.

The United States military shifted its defense bases from coastal areas to inland areas, including Arizona, during World War II.

The state has 160 radio stations to keep music and news flowing over Arizona's airwaves. There are about twenty-five state television stations.

Arizona is known for its high-quality golf clubs and tennis balls.

Arizona is home to some of the largest aviation manufacturing companies in the world.

Real estate is an important part of the service industry. The state's expanding population creates a constant demand for more houses and office buildings.

Some of Arizona's military bases include Davis-Monthan Air Force Base, Fort Huachuca Military Reservation, and Luke Air Force Base.

Arizonan Cesar Chavez dedicated his life to helping farm workers by establishing a union to protect workers' rights.

Nearly 500,000 Arizonans work in the service industry. Service **revenue** makes up the largest percentage of the total state income. Service workers are those who do something for someone else. Doctors, lawyers, and sales clerks are all members of the service sector. Other service providers support the state's strong tourism industry. Attractions such as the Grand Canyon and the state's many guest or **dude** ranches contribute to the success of the tourism industry.

Two of the state's largest employers are the Arizona State University and the University of Arizona. Many people have jobs at these educational facilities.

More than 600,000 people have taken mule tours into the Grand Canyon.

The University of Arizona employs more than 10,000 people.

FIRST NATIONS

Almost one-third of Arizona still belongs to Native Americans who have lived in the state for centuries. Among the earliest settlers were the Anasazi who lived in the north. Here, they grew corn, beans, squash, and cotton. They often built villages high up into the canyon walls, some of which can still be seen today. In the Gila and Salt River valleys, the Hohokam dug irrigation ditches to supply water to their desert fields, while the Mogollon lived and hunted in the east. In the 1400s, the Navajo and Apache came to Arizona. The Navajo grew crops and raised sheep in the northeast. The Apache hunted game in the southern mountains.

The hoop dance represents the cycles of life.

Many early Native Peoples in Arizona lived in pueblos. Pueblos were apartment-like structures with ladders connecting different levels.

As settlers moved into Arizona, many Native Peoples were forced from their land. In 1863, the United States army chased the Navajo out of their canyon homes and burned their crops.

Around 8,000 Navajo were captured and were forced to walk to New Mexico. This forced march is known in Navajo history as the "Long Walk." Finally, a new treaty was signed in 1868, and the surviving Navajo were allowed to go back to a reservation in their former territory.

While setting up a colony in New Mexico, Juan de Oñate and his men explored the surrounding territory and found silver deposits in Arizona.

EXPLORERS

By the 1500s, the Spanish had conquered Mexico. Soon after, they heard about incredible riches to the north. In 1539, Marcos de Niza led an **expedition** to find the legendary Seven Cities of Cìbola, which were said to have golden streets. Their search led them to Arizona. The next year, Francisco Vásquez de Coronado traveled through Arizona, also in search of these wealthy cities. One of his men set out to find the **fabled** Great River and came upon the Grand Canyon. The river running through it seemed like a stream, so he left unimpressed. Coronado continued searching for the cities all the way to Kansas before realizing that they were just a legend.

Over the next several decades, few expeditions traveled through Arizona. In 1595, Juan de Oñate was given permission to settle Arizona. Three years later, his expedition set out and took control of New Mexico, which included Arizona. Spaniards then began entering Arizona to search for silver deposits. They found silver near present-day Prescott.

QUICK FACTS

The first explorers to set foot in Arizona may have been part of an expedition led by Álvar Núñez Cabeza de Vaca from Spain. They were shipwrecked on the Texas coast in 1528. An epic eight-year journey to Mexico City resulted in the death of all but four members of the crew.

In 1582, Antonio de Espejo went to Arizona and found silver deposits near present-day Jerome. The samples he brought home increased interest in the area.

Francisco Vásquez de Coronado was accompanied by many Native Peoples and about 300 soldiers when he explored Arizona.

Along with his missionary work, Eusebio Kino made several maps of Arizona. These maps were used for more than 100 years.

MISSIONARIES

In 1629, Spanish missionaries arrived in Arizona at the Hopi mesas. They hoped to convert the Native Peoples to Christianity. Native Americans were forbidden to practice their own religion. By 1680, the Pueblo Native Peoples in New Mexico rebelled against the Spanish and drove them out of the area. The Hopi in Arizona followed suit. Missionaries never returned to that area again.

Missionaries had better luck in southern Arizona. A Spanish priest named Eusebio Kino taught Native Americans new ways to farm and raise cattle and sheep. He respected the Native Peoples. Kino set up twenty-four missions in southern Arizona and northern Mexico. When Kino died, the missionaries who replaced him were less kind. Soon, the Native Peoples rebelled against their demands. Efforts to establish missions in the area were abandoned.

The first mission that Father Eusebio Kino established in Arizona was the Tumacacori Mission.

QUICK FACTS

The Mission San Xavier Del Bac is the best-preserved mission church in the country. It was completed in 1797 near Tucson.

In 1768, Francisco Tomás Garcés began missionary work in Arizona. He went on to explore the Grand Canyon, visit Hopi villages, and find new routes to California.

Shortly after he arrived in Tombstone in 1879, Wyatt Earp became a United States Marshall for the Arizona Territory.

EARLY SETTLERS

In 1751, Native Americans clashed with Spanish settlers. In response, the Spanish built a military post at Tubac, which became Arizona's first non-Native American settlement. More military forts, including one at Tucson in 1775, were built to protect Spanish interests in the area. However, it was not long before the Spanish lost control of Arizona to Mexico.

In the 1820s, trappers, traders, and a few settlers from the United States began moving to Arizona. The United States and Mexico fought over territory, and United States troops claimed New Mexico, California, and part of Arizona in 1848. By 1853, the rest of Arizona had become United States territory.

Mining and farming prospects brought more settlers to Arizona. Phoenix emerged around the rebuilt Hohokam irrigation canals in 1867. People from all over the country flocked to Arizona to work in the mines and to farm.

Trading posts were not only places of business, but social centers as well. Along with goods, people would trade local news and gossip.

POPULATION

Arizona has the third-largest Native-American population in the United States. Only Oklahoma and California have more. About 250,000 Native Americans live in the state, mostly on one of twenty reservations. There are sixteen tribal councils that help govern Native-American groups and supervise their property.

While the majority of Arizonans are of European **ancestry**, about 18 percent are Hispanic Americans. Most trace their roots to Mexico, Puerto Rico, Cuba, Nicaragua, and Guatemala. African Americans comprise about 3 percent of Arizona's total population, and Asians and Pacific Islanders comprise about 1.5 percent.

In the 1970s, towns and cities accounted for about half of Arizona's population. Now, nearly 90 percent of Arizonans live in these **urban** areas. More than half of Arizona's population live in the Phoenix-Mesa area. Another one-fifth live in the resort region of Tucson.

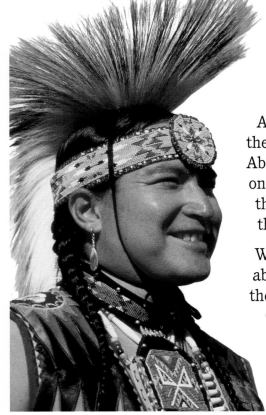

The Hopi have been living in the settlement of Oraibi in northern Arizona since the 1100s.

QUICK FACTS

Tucson has a population of about 449,000 people, and Mesa has about 344,700 people.

In 1900, Arizona's population was 100,000. By 1920 it reached 300,000. In 1940 it sat at 500,000, and by 1960 it broke the million mark with 1.3 million residents. Today, the population is approximately 4.8 million.

More than 1 million people in Arizona are less than 17 years of age.

Supreme Court Judge Sandra Day O'Connor grew up on a ranch in Arizona.

POLITICS AND GOVERNMENT

Arizona holds many firsts in politics and government. In 1981, Sandra Day O'Connor became the first female judge appointed to the United States Supreme Court. In 1988, the state became the first in history to elect women to the top five executive offices.

The Arizona government is structured much like the federal government—it has executive, legislative, and judicial branches. The executive branch is led by the governor, who is elected to a four-year term. The governor appoints officials, sets the budget, and decides which state issues are most important. New laws need to be approved in the executive before they are **enacted**. The legislative branch is composed of a Senate of thirty members and House of Representatives of sixty members. Here, new laws are introduced, and old ones are changed. The judicial branch consists of the courts. The highest court is the Arizona Supreme Court, and its judges are appointed to six-year terms.

QUICK FACTS

Arizona was the forty-eighth state to join the Union on February 14, 1912.

Rose Mofford became the state's first female governor in 1988.

Native Americans obtained the right to vote in 1948.

There is enough copper on the dome of the Arizona Capitol to make almost 5 million copper pennies.

CULTURAL GROUPS

More than 1 million Latin Americans call Arizona home. Their roots were firmly planted before Arizona had even reached statehood. Many people in southern Arizona are **bilingual**, capable of speaking both Spanish and English. On September 16, festivals celebrate Mexican Independence Day. Throughout the state, parties featuring **mariachi** bands and fireworks celebrate Mexico's successful fight for independence from Spain.

In Arizona, traditional dances are performed during Mexican Independence Day.

As a southern state, Arizona embraces cowboy culture. Many of the first cowboys were Mexican, and some of the cowboy terms used today have Mexican origins. *Vaquero* became "buckaroo" in English, *la reata* became "**lariat**," and *chaparreras* were leather leggings worn by cowboys—they are now known as "chaps." Tucson celebrates its Mexican cowboy culture during *La Fiesta de los Vaqueros*.

QUICK FACTS

Spanish and Mexican influences can be seen in the style of buildings and in place names.

Arizona's southern culture is shown in its choice of official state neckwear—the bola tie. This tie is a favorite among cowboys, and was invented in Arizona.

In Sedona, Mexican Independence Day is celebrated with Mexican arts and crafts, food, music, and dancing at the *Fiesta del Tlaquepaque*.

All Hopi children become members of the community through their mother's clan.

During the 1800s, many people from Ireland, Germany, Italy, and Serbia arrived in the state to work in copper mines. Some African Americans moved to Arizona to work on ranches. During the state's early days, many Chinese moved to the state to build railroads and work in mines. Other people of Asian background, including Japanese, Koreans, Vietnamese, and Laotians, have since moved to Arizona, enriching the state with their culture and traditions. Japanese culture is celebrated every year with the *Matsuri* festival. During this celebration, people can watch demonstrations of martial arts or the delicate art of paper folding, called *origami*.

Every September, the Navajo celebrate their traditions at the Navajo Nation Fair in Window Rock, the capital of the Navajo Reservation. It is the biggest Native-American fair in the world. Many people go to view rodeos, parades, and exhibits of jewelry, blankets, and other crafts.

QUICK FACTS

The vast majority of Native Americans in Arizona are Navajo.

The Navajo reservation, which is located in northeastern Arizona and parts of Utah and New Mexico, is about the size of West Virginia.

Of all the states, Arizona has the most land set aside for Native-American reservations.

Many Chinese people settled in towns in Arizona and established a variety of independent businesses.

Tucson's Irish community celebrates St. Patrick's Day with festivals and parades.

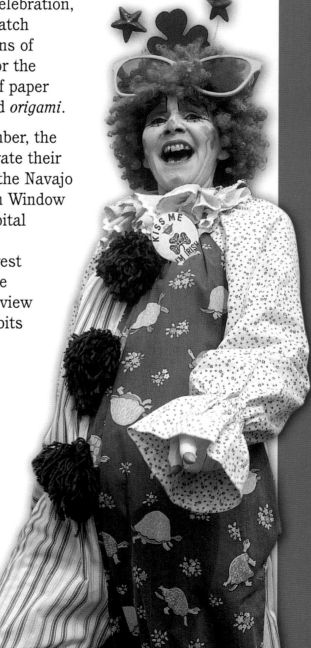

ARTS AND ENTERTAINMENT

A bronze statue of the Rough Riders of the Spanish American War stands proudly in Prescott.

Arizona's picturesque landscapes serve as inspiration to talented local artists. Thomas Moran was the first person to paint the Grand Canyon, as well as other popular state locations. His work is displayed in the nation's Capitol in Washington, D.C. Other artists, including Maynard Dixon and Frederic Remington, painted colorful scenes of Arizona during the early 1900s.

Arizona's Native-American population is known for its pottery, woven baskets, and blankets. Navajo blankets and rugs of every imaginable color are prized throughout the world. Native-American silversmiths have also gained recognition as creators of ornate jewelry.

One of the most celebrated western novelists captured the history and beauty of Arizona in his writing. Although born in Ohio, Zane Grey told many tales of western adventure set in Arizona. His novels continue to thrill fans. Another author, Oliver La Farge, wrote a Pulitzer prize-winning book, *Laughing Boy*, in the 1920s. This novel honors the Native Americans of Arizona.

Some Navajo pottery features traditional surface decorations. Paint shows the influence of Puebloan potters, since early Navajo pottery was not painted.

QUICK FACTS

Scottsdale has one of the country's highest concentrations of art galleries.

R. C. Gorman grew up on a Navajo reservation. This artist painted Native Americans, but did not use the traditional, flat style of his ancestors. He used simple lines instead.

The Heard Museum, in Phoenix, is a world-renowned museum devoted to Native American art and culture.

Zane Grey is credited with writing eighty-five books. Along with his western adventure novels, eight books are about Grey's fishing and hunting experiences.

For music buffs, Arizona's Phoenix Symphony Orchestra is sure to please. The Arizona Opera Company is the state's only professional opera group. Scottsdale hosts Jazz in Arizona concerts, Sedona puts on Jazz on the Rocks, and Tucson sponsors the Tucson Jazz Festival. Arizonans have made their mark in country and rock music as well. Marty Robbins, born in Glendale, was one of the most successful country musicians in the nation. Over the span of his long career, Robbins starred in his own television show and had ninety-four country chart hits. Linda Ronstadt, from Tucson, has also had many of her songs soar on the charts. She has won ten Grammy Awards, including one for a Spanish-language album in 1987.

Director Steven Spielberg was born in Ohio, but grew up in Scottsdale, Arizona. He began making movies when he was twelve. Spielberg directed three of the largest-grossing movies in Hollywood history—*Jurassic Park*, *E.T.*, and *Raiders of the Lost Ark*. In front of the camera, Ted Danson, who grew up in Flagstaff, kept *Cheers* fans entertained playing the role of the arrogant bartender, Sam Malone.

Steven Spielberg made his first movie at the age of 16. A local theater played it for one evening.

QUICK FACTS

Lynda Carter, star of the television show, *Wonder Woman*, was born in Phoenix.

Frank Lloyd Wright was a great architect. His home, studio, and school of architecture are in Paradise Valley near Scottsdale.

Tucson's La Fiesta de los Chiles delivers on its promise of a hot time. The food is very spicy, and features jalapeno and chili peppers.

More than 7,500 people attend the Sedona Jazz on the Rocks festival each year.

SPORTS

Arizona offers incredible opportunities for sports lovers. People can water-ski in the morning in 80°F weather and then bundle up for an afternoon of snow skiing on Mount Lemmon or the Fairfield Snowbowl. Rivers and lakes provide great fishing and boating locations for Arizonans. Because of the warm climate, Arizonans can bicycle, rock climb, swim, and jog throughout the year. Tennis, baseball, and hiking are other fun ways to spend time in Arizona.

Fishers in Arizona have hundreds of lakes from which to choose.

Golf is a favorite year-round activity in Arizona. In Phoenix, about 11 million rounds of golf are played every year on the city's 190 courses. Amateur golfers are not the only athletes to enjoy the stunning Arizona courses. The Professional Golf Association and the Ladies Professional Golf Association often visit Arizona courses during their tours.

Arizona's mild climate makes the state a mountain biker's paradise.

QUICK FACTS

Hot-air balloons fill the air during rallies that take place at Fountain Hills.

The first organized rodeo to offer prizes and charge admission was in Prescott in 1888. The "Cowboy Tournament" turned the rodeo into a spectator sport. The Prescott Rodeo is still held every year.

Olympic gold medal gymnast Kerri Strug is from Tucson. She captured hearts when she competed at the 1996 Olympics with a badly sprained ankle and torn **ligaments**.

There is no shortage of professional sports teams to cheer for in Arizona. In 1988, the state acquired its own professional football team—the Phoenix Cardinals. The team trains in Flagstaff during the summer and heads to Tempe's Sun Devil Stadium to tackle opponents during its home games.

Arizona's warm climate entices eight major-league baseball teams to Arizona for spring training. Professional teams include the Milwaukee Brewers, Cleveland Indians, Seattle Mariners, and the Chicago Cubs. Under the state's sunny skies, they work on their batting, fielding, and throwing skills. Once the regular season starts, the Arizona Diamondbacks, the state's homegrown team, thrill packed stadiums.

Professional basketball fans turn their eyes toward the sun, the Phoenix Suns that is. Since 1968, the Suns have wowed fans at the Arizona Veteran's Memorial Coliseum. Suns stars including Charles Barkley and Penny Hardaway have led the squad to many playoff championships. The Coliseum is also home to the Phoenix Coyotes of the National Hockey League.

Randy Johnson is one of only two pitchers in major league baseball history to strike out 300 batters three years in a row.

Large groups of fans come to the Arizona Veteran's Memorial Coliseum to cheer on the Coyotes.

QUICK FACTS

The Cardinals were in St. Louis before moving to Phoenix. The team is the oldest football franchise in the nation.

Helen Hull Jacobs was born in Globe. She was one of the twentieth century's greatest tennis players. She ranked among the top ten players in the world every year from 1928 until 1940.

Brain Teasers

1

TRUE OR FALSE?

There used to be volcanoes in Arizona.

Answer: True. There is evidence of volcanic eruptions at Chiricahua National Monument and Sunset Crater Volcano National Monument. The Turkey Creek Caldera eruption in Chiricahua was 1,000 times more powerful than the 1980 eruption of Mount Saint Helens.

2

What made the Apaches such great warriors?

Answer: Apaches were trained in warfare and were skilled horsemen. They operated from a range of difficult-to-reach hills in the southeast. Cochise and Geronimo were Apache leaders who are well known for evading settlers and soldiers.

3

What legendary Arizonan worked as a stagecoach driver, railroad construction worker, buffalo hunter, and surveyor as a young man?

Answer: Wyatt Earp. He later tried to tame the Wild West.

4

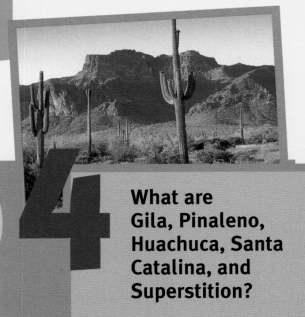

What are Gila, Pinaleno, Huachuca, Santa Catalina, and Superstition?

Answer: They are all mountain ranges in the Basin and Range region of Arizona.

5

TRUE OR FALSE?

Agave is a Native-American group in Arizona.

Answer: False. An Agave is a desert plant. The best known agave is the American aloe. It flowers only once when it is between 10 and 25 years old. Agaves have fleshy leaves that look like flattened bunches of green bananas.

6

How many flags have flown over Arizona through history?

Answer: There have been five flags to fly over the state. The Castilian and Burgundian flags of Spain, the Mexican flag, the Confederate flag, and the United States flag have all waved over Arizona.

7

Frank Lloyd Wright spent his winters in Scottsdale and died in Phoenix in 1959. What did he do that made him famous?

Answer: Frank Lloyd Wright was an important architect. He designed the Larkin Building in New York in 1904. It was the first office building to use air conditioning, double-glass windows, all-glass doors, and metal furniture.

8

How did the London Bridge end up in Arizona?

Answer: By 1962, London Bridge was falling apart due to all the traffic it supported over the Thames River. The British government decided to sell the bridge. Robert McCulloch, an Arizona businessperson, offered more than $2.4 million. His bid was accepted. The bridge was taken apart, and each stone was marked so it could be reassembled.

FOR MORE INFORMATION

Books

Fradin, Dennis Brindell. *From Sea to Shining Sea: Arizona.* Chicago: Children's Press, 1993.

Heinrichs, Ann. *America the Beautiful: Arizona.* Chicago: Children's Press, 1991.

McDaniel, Melissa. *Celebrate the States: Arizona.* New York: Benchmark Books, 2000.

Web sites

You can also go online and have a look at the following Web sites:

Arizona State Homepage
http://www.state.az.us

50 States: Arizona
http://www.50states.com

Tourism Arizona
http://www.arizonaguide.com

Lost in the Grand Canyon: The American Experience
http://www.pbs.org/wgbh/amex/canyon

Some Web sites stay current longer than others. Use your favorite search engine to find more about this state by entering keywords such as "Arizona," "Grand Canyon," "desert," "Diamondbacks," or any other topic you want to research.

GLOSSARY

ancestry: distant relatives

aviation: the design, development, and production of aircraft

bilingual: a person who is able to use two languages, especially with equal ability

butte: a tall column of rock

cargo: goods carried on a ship or plane

clan: a group of people of common descent

domestic: of one's own country

dude: a city-dweller who vacations on a ranch

enacted: made into law

expedition: a journey made for exploration

fabled: fictitious

gorge: narrow, steep-sided valley

hydroelectricity: water-generated power

irrigation: supplying land with water by using streams, canals, dams, and other methods

isolated: set apart or away from human contact

lariat: a rope used to tether a horse

ligaments: tough tissue that holds bones together or organs in place

mariachi: Mexican band

mesa: a flat-topped hill with cliff-like sides

petrified: stone-like

pueblos: communal homes built by Native Americans

revenue: income

urban: relating to city life

INDEX